P9-DIJ-186

AMERICA
THE BEAUTIFUL

SCHOLASTIC INC.

Cartwheel BOOKS

New York Toronto London Auckland Sydney Mexico City New Delhi Hong Kong

Photography credits for *America the Beautiful*:

Cover: top left: Joseph Sohm/Stone; top right: SuperStock; bottom right: SuperStock; bottom left: SuperStock

Back cover: Lori Adamski Peek/Stone

Pages: 2-3: Bob Rowan; Progressive Image/Corbis; 4-5: FPG; 6-7 background: Darrell Gulin; 6: W. Wayne Lockwood, M.D./Corbis; 7: Paul Stover/Stone; 8-9: SuperStock; 10: SuperStock; 11, top left: SuperStock; 11, top right: SuperStock; 11, bottom left: Stephanie Maze/Corbis; 12-13, background: Keven R. Morris/Corbis; 12, top row left: Michael Townsend/Stone; 12, top row middle: Cosmo Condina/Stone; 12, top row right: FPG; 12, middle row left: Joseph Pobereskin/Stone; 12, middle row right: Mike Zens/Corbis; 12, bottom row right: Steve Raymer/Corbis; 13, top left: SuperStock; 13, second row left: FPG; 13, second row center: David Muench/Stone; 13, second row right: Dallas and John Heaton/Corbis; 13, third row left, Wolfgang Kaehler/Corbis; 13, third row right: FPG; 13, bottom right: Toyohiro Yamada/FPG; 14-15: Doug Wilson/Corbis; 16: SuperStock; 17: Joseph Sohm/Stone; 18, top left: Harvey Lloyd/FPG; 18, bottom left: Lori Adamski Peek/Stone; 18, bottom right: Lori Adamski Peek/Stone; 19: Stephen Simpson/FPG; 20: Bruce Hands/Stone; 21: Jake Rajs/Stone; 22-23: Darrell Gulin/Stone; 24: David Young Wolff/PhotoEdit.

ISBN 0-439-33302-4

Copyright © 2001 by Scholastic Inc.
All rights reserved. Published by Scholastic Inc.
SCHOLASTIC, CARTWHEEL BOOKS, and associated logos are trademarks and/or registered trademarks of Scholastic Inc.

10 9 8 7 6 5 4 3 2 1   01 02 03 04 05

Printed in the U.S.A.   08
First printing, September 2001

O beautiful

For spacious skies,

For amber waves of grain,

For purple mountain majesties

Above the fruited plain!

America! America!

God shed his grace on thee,

And crown thy good

With brotherhood

From sea to shining sea!

O beautiful
For spacious skies,
For amber waves of grain,
For purple mountain majesties
Above the fruited plain!
America! America!
God shed his grace on thee,
And crown thy good
With brotherhood
From sea to shining sea!